To Parents and Teachers

This book was written to help middle and older elementary children become familiar with their Bibles and learn how to use them.

This is a self-instruction book, designed for a student to use alone at his or her own speed. To use the book, the student needs a NRSV Children's Bible published by Abingdon Press © 2006, Nashville, Tennessee. The student also needs a pencil with an eraser and a pair of scissors. Each individual needs her or his own copy of this book. The child will need to write answers on the pages where instructed to do so.

Since this book is intended for use with the Abingdon NRSV Children's Bible, a student might need assistance if using a different version of the Bible.

Younger, more inexperienced readers, require three to four hours to complete this book; whereas older, more experienced readers, might be able to complete this book in one to two hours

In order to effectively use this resource, a student must be able to use a Table of Contents; find page numbers as high as 900; and know the difference between a comma, a colon, and a semicolon when they are used in a Bible reference.

A student who has completed this book will be able to:

- Find any book in the Old or New Testaments using the Table of Contents.
- Find any chapter in any book and any verse in any chapter.
- Find parts of verses when the Bible reference uses the letters a, b, and c with a verse number.
- Tell the difference between books of the Bible with similar names such as 1 Samuel and 2 Samuel and John and 1 John.
- Recognize the additional helps in a Bible and be able to use them.

This resource can be used in a number of ways:

ɩt home during any time of day.

n the classroom.

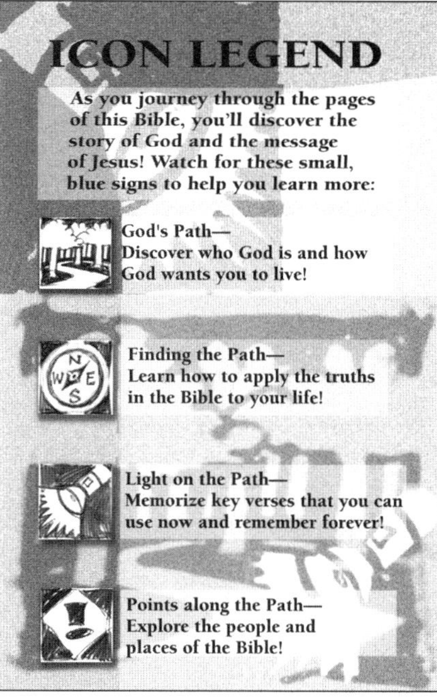

The Icon Legend will help you find:

1) God's Path. This will help you discover who God is and how God wants you to live.

2) Finding the Path. This will help you learn how to apply the truths in the Bible to your life.

3) Light on the Path. This icon alerts you that a certain verse can be memorized so that you can use it now and remember it forever.

4) Points along the Path. These help you explore the people and places of the Bible.

This book will help you use and enjoy the Bible.

This book is a different kind of book. It is something like a puzzle book. To use this book, you will need a NRSV Children's Bible (New Revised Standard Version Children's Bible), a pencil with an eraser on it, and

a pair of scissors.

IF YOU HAVE YOUR BIBLE, PENCIL, AND SCISSORS, THEN YOU CAN BEGIN USING THIS BOOK.

On each page, you will read something about your Bible.

Then you will read a sentence that has some words missing. Or maybe there will be a question.

Sometimes you will write the answer in a blank space like this: ____.

Sometimes your answer will have more than one word, and you will write in spaces like this: __________ __________ __________.

Or the answer may be started for you: (a _ _ _ _ _) and you will finish it like this: a n s w e r.

Sometimes you will check the right answer, like this:

_____ wrong answer

_____ right answer

LOOK IN THE GRAY STRIP AT THE LEFT SIDE OF THE NEXT PAGE.

map

HALLELUJAH!
THIS IS THE END OF THE BOOK.

NOW YOU KNOW HOW TO USE A BIBLE. YOU KNOW THAT EVERY BIBLE IS A LITTLE DIFFERENT, BUT YOU WILL KNOW THE THINGS YOU SHOULD SEARCH FOR IN ANY BIBLE AND HOW TO FIND MANY THINGS IN ANY BIBLE.

LOOK HERE FOR THE ANSWER:

The right answer will always be found in this gray strip at the left of the next page after the question.

Don't be surprised if a question is the same as a question you have already answered. Some of the questions will be asked again.

That makes the answers very EASY!

And by thinking of and writing the answer more than once, you will learn it and remember it for a long time.

Many of the questions are not hard but are E __ __ __.

THAT'S IT! TAKE YOUR PENCIL AND WRITE ONE LETTER IN EACH BLANK!

NOW LOOK AT THE LEFT SIDE OF THE NEXT PAGE TO CHECK YOUR ANSWER.

167

bottom

footnote

168

If you want to find where a city, country, lake, river, or sea mentioned in the Bible is located, you would look on a m__ __ found in the Bible.

5

SEE! YOU GOT THIS ANSWER RIGHT!

E A S Y

6

Sometimes this book will tell you to look for things in the Bible. Then you will stop reading this book and look in your BIBLE.

When you have found what you are looking for in your Bible, you will come back to this book to see if you have found the right thing.

This book will help you learn to use your B __ __ __ __.

YOU KNOW THAT WORD. IT TELLS THE STORIES OF GOD'S PEOPLE!

REMEMBER TO CHECK YOUR ANSWER ON THE NEXT PAGE.

Dictionary

When you see a little letter (like *a*, *b*, *h*, or *m*) by a word as you read in the Bible, you know that it tells you to look at the ____________________ of the page if you want to learn more.

When you look there, you will find a ____________________ with more information.

ISN'T THIS EASY?

B I B L E

BUT BE CAREFUL!

In order to learn how to find things in your Bible, be sure to read every line on each page in this book and DO EVERYTHING THE BOOK TELLS YOU TO DO.

By the time you reach the end of this book, you will know how to use your ____________________ very well.

CHECK YOUR ANSWER.

Bible Basics

If you do not understand a word in your Bible, you can look in the Bible ______________________.

BIBLE

Another different thing about this book is that when you are finished reading all the pages that go this way, then you turn the book around and read the rest of the pages.

THIS IS A VERY DIFFERENT AND INTERESTING BOOK!

Now you are ready to begin learning how to find certain things in your ______________________.
You will learn how to use your ________________ so that you can use it every single day of your life!

First

12

second

31

14

first 1

In the NRSV Children's Bible, there is a section in the front of the Bible called B__________ B___________.

This section talks about what the Bible is, who wrote the Bible, when it was written, why the Bible is important to people today, and how you can find your way through the Bible.

BIBLE

BIBLE

The Bible looks like one big book.

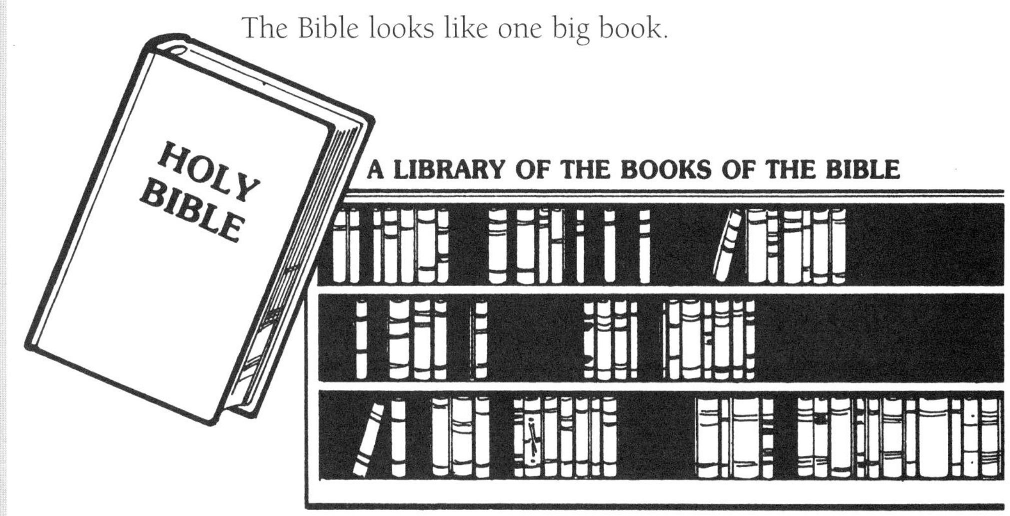

But it really is a lot of smaller books put together. It is like a library full of books.

Did you know that the word BIBLE means BOOKS?

Another word for “books” is __ __ __ __ __.

First

The Bible reference:

1 CORINTHIANS 12:31b through 14:1a

means that you find ________________ Corinthians, Chapter ________________.

You begin reading at the ______________________ part of verse __________ and read to the end of Chapter 13.

Then you read on into Chapter __________ to the end of the ________________ part of verse __________.

BIBLE

When you say the word "Bible," you are actually talking about a lot of smaller ___ ___ ___ ___ ___ put together into one big book.

162

second

163

In the Bible reference 1 SAMUEL, the number 1 in the name means that you are to find ______________________ Samuel.

B O O K S

The word "Bible" means ______________________.

REMEMBER THIS,
BECAUSE YOU WILL BE
ASKED THIS QUESTION
AGAIN AND AGAIN.
YOU CAN REMEMBER IT!

161

first

162

In the Bible reference MATTHEW 28:20b, the “b” after the “20” means that you read the ____________________ part of verse 20.

books

The Bible is called "Bible" because it is not just one big book, but it is a lot of smaller ______________________ with one cover.

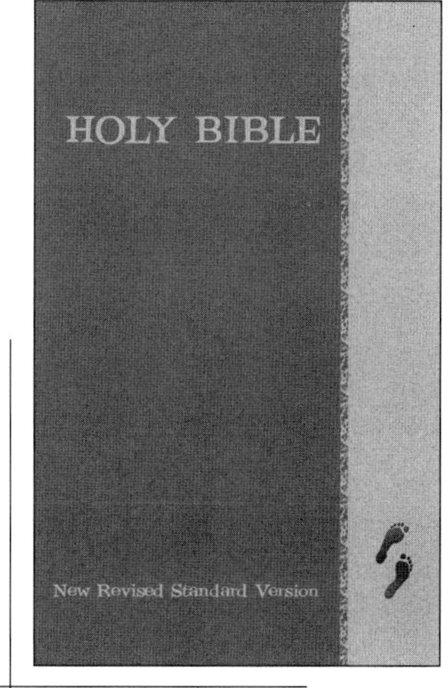

1 1 8

19

14 15

In the Bible reference MATTHEW 28:19a, the “a” after the “19” means that you read only the ________________ part of verse 19.

books

The word "Bible" means ______________________________.

skip

In the Bible reference JEREMIAH 1:1-8; 19:14-15, first you read Chapter __________, verses ___________ through __________.

Then you skip to Chapter __________ and read verses __________ and __________.

books

SEE! WE ASKED YOU THE SAME QUESTION AGAIN. I BET YOU LEARNED THE ANSWER!

This is a picture of a page near the front of the Bible.

Draw a circle around the words in this picture that say OLD AND NEW TESTAMENTS.

See if you can find this page in your Bible.

THE NRSV
CHILDREN'S BIBLE

containing the
Old and New Testaments

New Revised Standard Version

Abingdon Press
Nashville

21

37

22 1

In the Bible reference COLOSSIANS 3:17, 23-24

the comma (,) means that you

_____ read all the verses between 17 and 23.

or

_____ skip all the verses between 17 and 23.

(Check the right word.)

THE NRSV
CHILDREN'S BIBLE

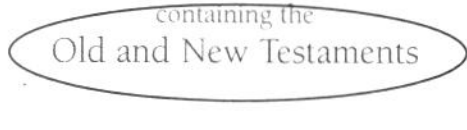

New Revised Standard Version

Abingdon Press

If you had a hard time finding this page in your Bible, ask someone for help.

The words "Old and New Testaments" tell you that there are two MAIN PARTS in the Bible: the O__________ and N___________ Testaments.

157

1 6

read

The Bible reference LUKE 21:37 through 22:1 means that you are to find the Book of Luke, Chapter __________, and begin reading at verse __________.

When you finish that chapter, you keep on reading in Chapter __________ to the end of verse __________.

OLD NEW

Can you find how many books of the Bible there are?

____

We have learned that the Bible is a collection of books. These books were stories that people told from memory. Parents told these stories about God's people to their children who told them to their children. Later, the stories were written down.

Before the stories were written down, how did the stories spread? The stories were told by M __ M __ __ __.

verse

In the Bible reference MARK 3:1-6, you read from the beginning of verse __________ to the end of verse __________.

The hyphen (-) means you

_____ (read) all the verses between 1 and 6.

or

_____ (skip) all the verses between 1 and 6.

66

MEMORY

The Bible is a gift to us from God. As we read the Bible, we learn more about God's great love for all people and how Jesus taught us to live.

The Bible is a gift to us from ___ ___ ___.

The Bible tells us how Jesus wants us to ___ ___ ___ ___.

155

chapter

156

In the Bible reference: LUKE 2:14,

the number "14" is the _____ (verse) number.

or

_____ (chapter) number.

GOD

LIVE

The name of one large group of books in the Bible is the OLD Testament.

A second large group of books in the Bible is called the ____________ Testament.

154

verses

155

In the Bible reference: LUKE 2:14

the number "2" is the _____ (verse) number.

or

_____ (chapter) number.

(Check the right word.)

NEW

A list of the books of the Bible is found in every Bible. Open your Bible. You will have to turn the pages until you find a page that looks like this:

Names and Order of the Books of the Bible

The Old Testament

Genesis	1	Ecclesiastes	767
Exodus	63	Song of Solomon	778
Leviticus	115	Isaiah	786
Numbers	151	Jeremiah	863
Deuteronomy	201	Lamentations	938
Joshua	246	Ezekiel	947
Judges	276	Daniel	1008
Ruth	308	Hosea	1028
1 Samuel	314	Joel	1042
2 Samuel	354	Amos	1048
1 Kings	388	Obadiah	1060
2 Kings	427	Jonah	1063
1 Chronicles	464	Micah	1067
2 Chronicles	498	Nahum	1076
Ezra	540	Habakkuk	1080
Nehemiah	554	Zephaniah	1085
Esther	572	Haggai	1090
Job	584	Zechariah	1093
Psalms	626	Malachi	1105
Proverbs	732		

The New Testament

Matthew	1109	1 Timothy	1384
Mark	1152	2 Timothy	1390
Luke	1180	Titus	1395
John	1225	Philemon	1398
Acts	1258	Hebrews	1401
Romans	1301	James	1415
1 Corinthians	1320	1 Peter	1421
2 Corinthians	1338	2 Peter	1427
Galatians	1350	1 John	1431
Ephesians	1357	2 John	1437
Philippians	1364	3 John	1439
Colossians	1370	Jude	1441
1 Thessalonians	1375	Revelation	1444
2 Thessalonians	1380		

The list of books is in two parts:

The Books of the ________________ Testament

The Books of the ________________ Testament

153

chapters

154

In the Bible, the chapters have been divided into small parts called ______________________.

Old New

or

New Old

(either way is right)

Now find the name of the SECOND book in the OLD Testament list.

Write that name here: __ __ __ __ __ __

Cut out this bookmark and keep it at the page that says "Names and Order of the Books of the Bible."

THE BOOKS *of* THE BIBLE

God's

Finding

Light

Points

Most of the books of the Bible have been divided into large parts called ____________________.

EXODUS

Now see if you can find the Book of RUTH. It is also in the Old Testament list.

Ruth is _______ (eight) or _______ (ten) books down on the Old Testament list.

Check the right number.

151

Old
New

or

New
Old

152

In the NRSV Children's Bible, there is an Icon Legend. The four Icons are: 1) _ _ _ _ Path. 2) _ _ _ _ _ _ _ the Path. 3) _ _ _ _ _ on the Path. 4) _ _ _ _ _ _ along the Path.

eight

Lay a ruler or a pencil across the page under the name of the Book of Ruth.

Names and Order of the Books of the Bible

The Old Testament

Book	Page	Book	Page
Genesis	1	Ecclesiastes	767
Exodus	63	Song of Solomon	778
Leviticus	115	Isaiah	786
Numbers	151	Jeremiah	863
Deuteronomy	201	Lamentations	938
Joshua	246	Ezekiel	947
Judges	276	Daniel	1008
Ruth	308	Hosea	1028
1 Samuel	314	Joel	1042
2 Samuel	354	Amos	1048
1 Kings	388	Obadiah	1060
2 Kings	427	Jonah	1063
1 Chronicles	464	Micah	1067
2 Chronicles	498	Nahum	1076
Ezra	540	Habakkuk	1080
Nehemiah	554	Zephaniah	1085
Esther	572	Haggai	1090
Job	584	Zechariah	1093
Psalms	626	Malachi	1105
Proverbs	732		

The New Testament

Book	Page	Book	Page
Matthew	1109	1 Timothy	1384
Mark	1152	2 Timothy	1390
Luke	1180	Titus	1395
John	1225	Philemon	1398
Acts	1258	Hebrews	1401
Romans	1301	James	1415
1 Corinthians	1320	1 Peter	1421
2 Corinthians	1338	2 Peter	1427
Galatians	1350	1 John	1431
Ephesians	1357	2 John	1437
Philippians	1364	3 John	1439
Colossians	1370	Jude	1441
1 Thessalonians	1375	Revelation	1444
2 Thessalonians	1380		

In YOUR Bible, the Book of Ruth begins on page __________.

Turn to the Book of Ruth in your Bible, and keep the place.

DID YOU FIND THE BOOK OF RUTH IN YOUR BIBLE?

150

two

151

One of these two main parts of the Bible is called the

________________ Testament.

The other main part of the Bible is called the

________________ Testament.

Be sure that you found the correct page in your Bible and that you found the Book of Ruth. It might begin on page 308!

Ruth

The book of Ruth is about the relationship between a mother (in-law) and a daughter (in-law). This book tells the story of Ruth the Moabite who left Moab and her family to follow her mother-in-law, Naomi, to Bethlehem. Because Ruth trusted Naomi's God, she found a new home for herself and Naomi by marrying an Israelite named Boaz. The book of Ruth was written about 400 B.C., after the Jews who had been living in Babylon returned to Judah.

When Ruth was written, some leaders believed that Jews should not marry people from other cultures. The books of Ezra and Nehemiah show this belief. Other books show the tradition of caring for family, widows, and foreigners (Deuteronomy 24:19 and Leviticus 19:9-10; 25:25-34, 47-55). The author of the book of Ruth used the story of Ruth's marriage to Boaz to show that marriage with foreigners had long been accepted. This book is a call for people to treat one another with kindness and love. The writer used the story of Ruth to show the people that they needed to accept everyone and treat them with love.

God took care of Ruth and her mother-in-law, Naomi. Ruth and Boaz became the great-grandparents of the best-loved king of Israel and Judah, King David. The Gospel of Matthew, the first book in the New Testament, names the family of Jesus through David, and also through Ruth and Boaz.

Ruth 2:8-9

Look at where the story of Ruth begins. Find the words that say, "In the days when the judges ruled, there was a famine in the land, and a certain man of Bethlehem in Judah went to live in the country of Moab, he and his wife and two sons."

Find the missing word:

"In the __________ when the judges ruled, there was a famine in the land, and a certain man of Bethlehem in Judah went to live in the country of Moab, he and his wife and two sons."

Sometimes on a page before a Book of the Bible begins, there is information about the Book that explains when the book was written and by whom. Is there a page like that in your Bible?

149

books

150

The Bible has ____________________ main parts.

days

YOU ARE LEARNING FAST! YOU HAVE JUST LOOKED UP A BOOK IN THE BIBLE!

Now let us find another book in the Old Testament. Let us find the Book of JOB.

THE BOOK OF JOB SOUNDS LIKE "ROBE."

Look down the list of books in the front of your Bible until you come to the name "Job."

Find where the actual Book of Job begins. The Book of Job begins: There was once a

____________________ . . . ."

(Fill in the missing word.)

REMEMBER: YOU MIGHT HAVE AN INTRODUCTION PAGE ABOUT THE BOOK OF JOB BEFORE THE BOOK ACTUALLY BEGINS.

books

The Bible is called "Bible" because it is not just one big book, but a lot of smaller ________________ with one cover.

man

(If you did not find the Book of Job, look for it again. It is in the Old Testament.)

Let us find one more book in the Old Testament.

See if you can find the Book of JONAH.

The Book of Jonah begins, "Now the word of the __________ came to Jonah . . . ."

REMEMBER:
YOU MIGHT HAVE AN INTRODUCTION PAGE ABOUT THE BOOK OF JONAH BEFORE THE BOOK ACTUALLY BEGINS.

The word “Bible” means ______________________________.

LORD

(If you did not find the Book of Jonah in your Bible, ask someone to help you before you go any further.)

If you would like to stand up and stretch, this would be a good time.

But first, cut out the bookmark below and put it in this book so you will know where to begin again after you rest.

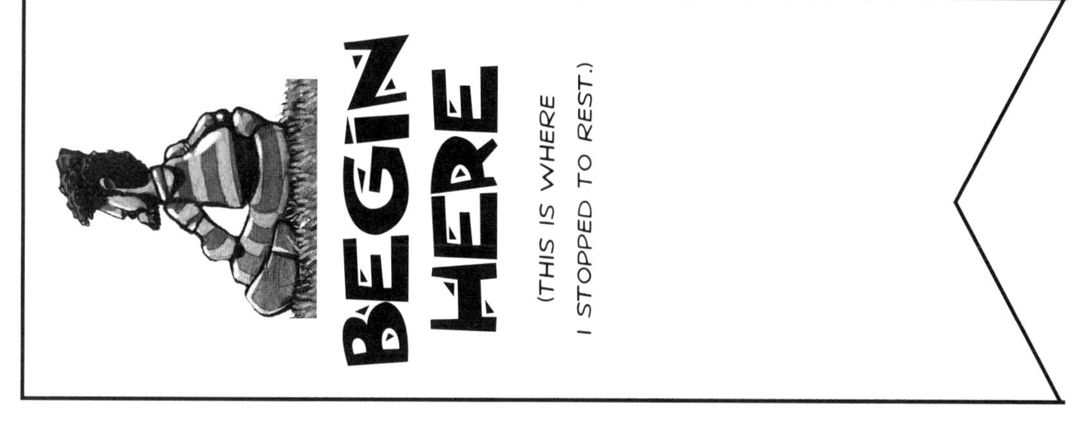

Matthew

Mark

Luke

John

HOORAY! YOU'VE ALMOST REACHED THE END OF THE BOOK! REST AWHILE, AND THEN SEE HOW MUCH YOU REMEMBER BY ANSWERING THE QUESTIONS ON THE FOLLOWING PAGES.
SEE HOW MANY YOU GET RIGHT.

ARE YOU READY
TO GO AGAIN?
LET US SEE WHAT
WE HAVE LEARNED
SO FAR AND THEN
LET US LEARN
SOME MORE.

The word "Bible" means

_______________________________.

GOOD NEWS

Write the names of the four Gospels of the New Testament:

____________________ ____________________

____________________ ____________________

books

If you have a New Revised Standard Version Children's Bible by Abingdon Press, you have an Icon Legend page near the front of your Bible. It tells you that there are four icons (markers) that will tell you something about the story of God and the message of Jesus. Look for the blue signs.

God's Path. Discover who God is and how God wants you to live!

Finding the Path. Learn how to apply the truths in the Bible to your life!

fish

bread

Do you know what the word GOSPEL means? Read the first two sentences of the blue information page before the Book of Matthew.

The word GOSPEL means G__________ N___________.

The first four books of the New Testament are called The GOSPELS. These books tell us the good news of Jesus Christ.

Matthew

The first four books of the New Testament are called Gospels. The word *gospel* means "good news." These books tell us the good news that Jesus came to earth to live as a human and to show us how we ought to live as the children of God. Each of the four books was written for a different group of readers, and the Gospel of Matthew was especially for Jews. This Gospel was written about 85 AD and was named for Matthew because he had collected some of the information about Jesus that went into the book.

Although the Gospel of Matthew is the first book in the New Testament, many people believe it was the third Gospel to be written. The writer used the Gospel of Mark as the main outline of the events of Jesus's life. In fact, the Gospel of Matthew quotes much of the Gospel of Mark.

The Gospel of Matthew tells the story of Jesus—his birth, life as an adult (including his ministry and teaching), crucifixion, and resurrection. This Gospel was written to encourage readers to have faith in Jesus as the Messiah (or "Christ," in Greek). The Gospel often makes connections between Jesus's teachings and the Hebrew Scriptures, which are what we call the Old Testament. The writer of the Gospel of Matthew wanted those who read or heard the Gospel to understand Jesus based on their knowledge of the Hebrew Scriptures.

Matthew 14:13–21

Light on the Path. Memorize key verses that you can use now and remember forever!

Points along the Path. Explore the people and places of the Bible!

The Bible has __________ main parts.

One of these two main parts of the Bible is called the __________ Testament.

musical

Let's find the Book of Matthew in your Bible. In many Bibles, including the NRSV Children's Bible, there is a page that gives information about the book. In the NRSV Children's Bible, it is a blue page. See if you can find the blue introduction page before the Book of Matthew begins. This page tells who wrote the book, when it was written, and what the book is about.

There is also a picture on the blue introduction page that tells about something that happens in the book.

On the blue introduction page before the Book of Matthew, you see two baskets. One basket is full of f __ __ __, and the other basket is full of b __ __ __ d.

two

Old or New

(either one is correct)

Now find the last book in the Old Testament.

Find the Book of MALACHI.

The Book of Malachi begins:

"An oracle. The ___________ of the Lord . . . ."

(Keep your Bible open to the Book of Malachi.)

Dictionary

Let's find a word in your Bible Dictionary.

Look up the word HARP in your Bible Dictionary.

A HARP is:

A stringed ______________________ instrument small enough to be carried.

word

Your Bible is open to the Book of Malachi, the last book in the Old Testament.

If you turn about four pages (depending on your version of the Bible), you will find a page that looks something like this:

THE NEW COVENANT
commonly called
THE NEW TESTAMENT
of
OUR LORD AND SAVIOR
JESUS CHRIST

New Revised Standard Version

141

The answers will vary.
In the NRSV Children's
Bible, the answer is 21.

142

A Bible DICTIONARY tells you what some of the words in the Bible mean.

If you do not understand a word, look in the Bible DICTIONARY to find what it means.

If you do not understand a word in your Bible, you can look in the Bible D ___ ___ ___ ___ ___ ___ ___ ___ ___.

(Fill in the missing letters.)

You found a page that looks something like this:

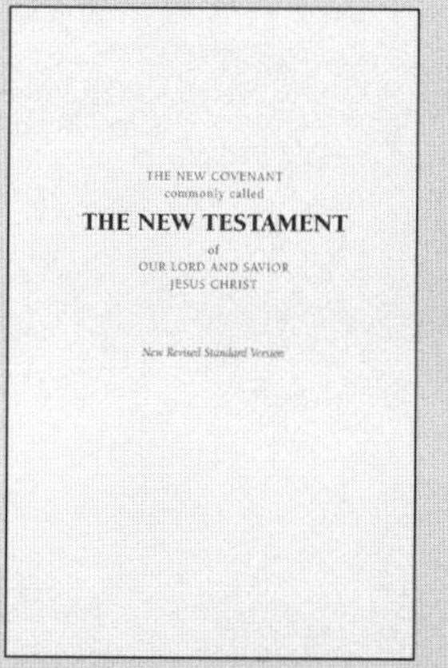

THE NEW COVENANT
commonly called
THE NEW TESTAMENT
of
OUR LORD AND SAVIOR
JESUS CHRIST

New Revised Standard Version

In many Bibles, the New Testament starts over again with page 1 and has another set of page numbers. In the *NRSV Children's Bible,* the New Testament begins on page 1110.

Cut out this bookmark and keep it at the page that says "The New Testament."

When you want to find a book in the New Testament, this bookmark will show you where to begin looking.

Matthew 14:22-33

We've talked about Bible dictionaries before. Let's talk about them again. Do you know what a dictionary is? A DICTIONARY is a special book that tells you what words mean.

Many Bibles have a dictionary.

How many pages in your Bible are dictionary pages?

____

Dictionary

A

Abba—An Aramaic word meaning "the father," "my father," or "our father." Jesus used this word as a familiar name for God, the Father.

abyss—An unmeasured, deep, bottomless pit.

adultery—Intimate and sinful physical relations between a married man and a woman who is not his wife, or between a married woman and a man who is not her husband.

alabaster—A soft stone, light and creamy in color and often having a striped appearance. In Bible times, people used alabaster for vases and flasks or for boxes to hold perfume and precious ointments.

allotment—In early Old Testament times, the portion of land given to each of the tribes occupying Canaan.

Almighty—Having all power. A name used to describe God's greatness, power, and might.

alms—Gifts given to the poor.

Alpha and Omega—The first and last letters of the Greek alphabet. In the New Testament, the letters are used together as symbols for God and Jesus Christ.

altar—A stone or pile of stones on which sacrifices were offered to God.

ambush—Waiting in a hiding place in order to attack an enemy by surprise.

Amen—A Hebrew word meaning "truly" or "surely." This word is often used at the end of songs or prayers.

angel—A spiritual being or messenger from God sometimes said to appear in human form.

anoint—To pour oil on the head or body of a person or on an object. In biblical times, anointing was often part of a religious ceremony showing that a person had been set apart for the service of the Lord.

antichrist—An enemy of Christ.

apostle—A title meaning "messenger" or "someone who is sent." The title given to the twelve disciples sent out by Jesus. Also refers to Paul and to other leaders in the early church. See also **disciple**.

Aramaic—A language closely related to Hebrew. During the time of Jesus, Aramaic was the everyday language of the Jews.

archangel—A chief angel.

Ark of the Covenant—A wooden box covered with gold that held the stone tablets containing the Ten Commandments. The Israelites carried the Ark with them during their wanderings in the wilderness, and they later placed the Ark in the Temple.

ark of Noah—A floating vessel like a houseboat in which Noah, his family, and at least one pair each of all living creatures took refuge during the Great Flood.

armlet—A metal ring or band worn on the upper arm as jewelry. Kings and other persons in authority wore armlets.

armor—Protective equipment given to soldiers to protect them during battle. The phrase "armor of God" is a way of speaking of the protection God gives people to stand against evil.

ascend—To go up. Forty days after Jesus's resurrection, he ascended into heaven.

atonement—The achievement of a state of harmony, or the overcoming of conflict or separation. People are separated from God due to their sin, and atonement (or reconciliation) brings agreement and restoration between people and God.

BE SURE YOU PUT THE BOOKMARK AT THE PAGE THAT SAYS "THE NEW TESTAMENT." LET THE BOOKMARK STICK OUT A BIT SO YOU CAN FIND THE PAGE EASILY.

The first book in the NEW Testament is the Book of

_______________________.

Answers will vary. Some important days of the Christian Year are:

1. Christmas Day
2. Day of Epiphany
3. Ash Wednesday
4. Palm Sunday
5. Easter Day
6. Ascension Sunday
7. Day of Pentecost
8. Trinity Sunday
9. All Saints Day
10. Christ the King Sunday

In many Bibles, there is an index that tells where to find stories or parts of the Bible.

Where can you find the story of Jesus walking on the water?

____

Matthew

Turn to the Book of MATTHEW in your Bible.

If you have a blue introduction page in your Bible, you will find information on the page just before the beginning of the Book of Matthew that tells you that the Book of Matthew is referred to as a G ___ S ___ E ___.

LUKE

PAUL

Eutychus

Some Bibles show the cycle of the Christian Year. Look in your Bible and see if you can find a Cycle of the Christian Year. Name three important days of the Christian Year.

1. ______________________

2. ______________________

3. ______________________

Now find another NEW Testament book.

Find the Book of ROMANS.

At the beginning of the Book of Romans, you will find information that says this book of the Bible was a letter that Paul wrote to the church in Rome.

This book is sometimes referred to as:

The Letter of P ___ u ___ to the R ___ m ___ n ___.

MATTHEW

BEATITUDES

Quite often, Bibles tell you more information about certain Bible people than you find in the Bible story. Does your Bible tell you information about Joanna? What do you learn about her? You can find two stories about Joanna in ___ U ___ ___ 8:1-3 and 24:1-12.

There is a story in the Bible about a man who became sleepy and fell out of a window while listening to P ___ ___ L preach. Look in Acts 20:9-10. What was the name of the man? ______________________________

Paul Romans

Sometimes two or more books in the Bible have almost the same name, like 1 SAMUEL and 2 SAMUEL. (We say "First Samuel" and "Second Samuel.")

The number at the front of the book helps you tell them apart. Look up the Old Testament book 1 SAMUEL.

BE CAREFUL! WATCH FOR THE NUMBER 1 IN THE NAME.

Do you remember how we say 1 SAMUEL?

__________ Samuel

sling

fishing

Ten Commandments

Sometimes in Bibles, very important parts of the Bible or very important teachings of Jesus are in a special place for people to read. One important prayer that Jesus taught is the Lord's Prayer. You might be able to find it in the middle of your Bible. You can also find the Lord's Prayer in M __ T __ H __ W 6:9-13. Read it out loud. Say it every night before you go to sleep, and think about what it means.

Do you know what the Beatitudes are? They are special teachings of Jesus that tell us how to be happy. Sometimes they are displayed in places such as in the middle of Bibles. You can also find The BEATI__ __ __ __ __ in Matthew 5:1-12. Think about what The Beatitudes mean.

First

Now look up the book 2 SAMUEL.

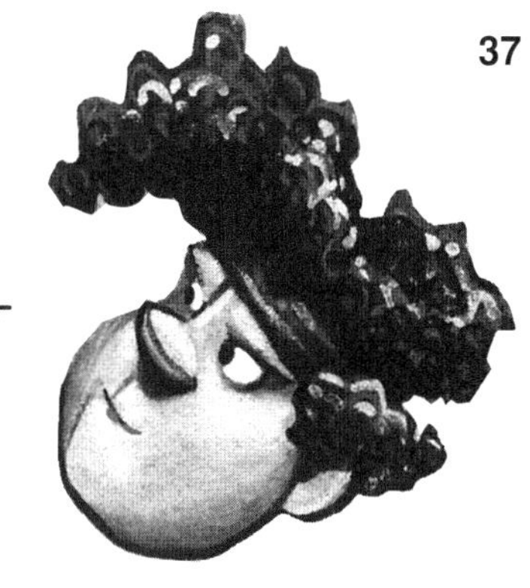
NOTICE THAT
IT FOLLOWS
1 SAMUEL.

Do you remember how we say 2 SAMUEL?

________________ Samuel

Now you know that there are two books of Samuel:

__________ Samuel

and

__________ Samuel

trumpet

lyre

jar

When David met Goliath face-to-face in 1 SAMUEL 17:40, he had a ________________ and five stones.

If you look in MARK 1:16-19, you will see that fishermen used something called ________________ nets.

If you look in EXODUS 20:1-17, you will find the T__ __ ____________________________.

Second

First

Second

How do you SAY the name of the book 1 SAMUEL?

Check the right answer:

_____ One Samuel

_____ First Samuel

How do you SAY the name of the book 2 SAMUEL?

_____ Second Samuel

_____ Two Samuel

maps

If you have a NRSV Children's Bible, you can find some of these Study Helps in your Bible. Turn to the Book of Malachi. It is the last book of the Old Testament. At the end of Malachi, you will find some very colorful pages that give you information about certain items you will find in Bible stories.

If you look in JOSHUA 6:4, you will find what a *shofar* is. It is a ________________ made of a ram's horn. It was and still is blown at Jewish ceremonies.

If you look in 1 SAMUEL 16:23, you will see that David played the _______________ before King Saul. A *lyre* was a musical instrument, much like a harp.

If you look in MARK 14:3, you will find that a woman poured ointment on Jesus' head from a __________ of oil.

First

Second

When you see the name of the book 2 SAMUEL, you know that the number 2 in the name means that you are to find ________________ Samuel (2 Samuel) instead of FIRST Samuel (1 Samuel.)

Bible Basics

What is the Bible?

The Bible is a very special collection of books filled with stories of God's love for people. It is a library you can hold in your hand! The sixty-six books of the Bible tell about God, the Creator of the universe, who made people and wanted them to follow God's ways. They tell about God's great love and that God sent Jesus to be the Savior of the people of the whole world. The Bible is a special book that shows us what God is like and how we can know God. The Bible comes from God, who inspired people to write down God's teachings, and who inspires us to read and understand God's teachings. Throughout history, the Bible has changed many people's lives. Through the Bible, God speaks to us today.

Who wrote the Bible, and when was it written?

The Bible is a collection of books that were written by many different people. Long ago, before there were written Bible stories, people told the stories from memory. Parents told them to their children, who told them to their children. God helped the people remember the stories and teachings. Later, people began to write the stories and teachings down. We believe that God inspired people to write the Bible teachings. (*Inspire* means that God's spirit helps us know the right thing to do.)

The stories and teachings of the Old Testament were told for hundreds of years before they were written. About 950 BC people began to write down some of the Old Testament stories. The Old Testament was first written in the Hebrew language.

The stories and teachings of the New Testament were also told for many years before they were written. Some of the New Testament letters were written about twenty-five years after Jesus died. Then, about thirty years after Jesus died, people began to write down the stories and teachings of Jesus that are included in the four Gospel books—Matthew, Mark, Luke, and John. The New Testament was first written in the Greek language.

The stories and teachings of our Bible have been told for thousands of years. The Bible message spread to many lands and into many languages. Jesus told his followers to go into all the world to preach, baptize, and teach. They obeyed, and the Good News of Jesus spread from town to town, from country to country, and from continent to continent. It took many people and thousands of years for the stories, songs, and messages of the Bible to be written. Today, the Bible is read in almost two thousand languages and in hundreds of countries.

Why is the Bible important to people today?

The Bible message is a gift to us from God. It is also a gift to us from many people. It took many years and many people to give us this gift! As we read our Bibles, we learn more about God's great love for all people and how Jesus taught us to live. The

Many times you will want to see where a city, town, river, or sea is located. You can find these places on a map. Finding these places might help you understand a Bible story better. You will definitely need a Bible MAP.

Maps in Bibles can be found in several locations. Often they are at the front or the back of a Bible.

Most Bibles have ________________ to help you find where a city, town, river, or sea is located.

Second

There is a book in the New Testament called 1 PETER.

REMEMBER, WE SAY "FIRST PETER."

There is another book in the New Testament with a name very much like 1 PETER. Can you guess its name? Try, and write it here:

_____ ________________

footnotes

Most Bibles have extra pages called STUDY HELPS or BIBLE BASICS that give information about the Bible, how the Bible was written, why the Bible is important to people today, how to find one's way through the Bible, a description of the books of the Bible, how to find specific Bible verses or passages, and what is a good way to begin reading the Bible. If you have a NRSV Children's Bible, you have all these topics.

Here is a picture of BIBLE BASICS found in the front of a Bible. Draw a circle around the words BIBLE BASICS.

Bible Basics

What is the Bible?

The Bible is a very special collection of books filled with stories of God's love for people. It is a library you can hold in your hand! The sixty-six books of the Bible tell about God, the Creator of the universe, who made people and wanted them to follow God's ways. They tell about God's great love and that God sent Jesus to be the Savior of the people of the whole world. The Bible is a special book that shows us what God is like and how we can know God. The Bible comes from God, who inspired people to write down God's teachings, and who inspires us to read and understand God's teachings. Throughout history, the Bible has changed many people's lives. Through the Bible, God speaks to us today.

Who wrote the Bible, and when was it written?

The Bible is a collection of books that were written by many different people. Long ago, before there were written Bible stories, people told the stories from memory. Parents told them to their children, who told them to their children. God helped the people remember the stories and teachings. Later, people began to write the stories and teachings down. We believe that God inspired people to write the Bible teachings. (*Inspire* means that God's spirit helps us know the right thing to do.)

The stories and teachings of the Old Testament were told for hundreds of years before they were written. About 950 BC people began to write down some of the Old Testament stories. The Old Testament was first written in the Hebrew language.

The stories and teachings of the New Testament were also told for many years before they were written. Some of the New Testament letters were written about twenty-five years after Jesus died. Then, about thirty years after Jesus died, people began to write down the stories and teachings of Jesus that are included in the four Gospel books—Matthew, Mark, Luke, and John. The New Testament was first written in the Greek language.

The stories and teachings of our Bible have been told for thousands of years. The Bible message spread to many lands and into many languages. Jesus told his followers to go into all the world to preach, baptize, and teach. They obeyed, and the Good News of Jesus spread from town to town, from country to country, and from continent to continent. It took many people and thousands of years for the stories, songs, and messages of the Bible to be written. Today, the Bible is read in almost two thousand languages and in hundreds of countries.

Why is the Bible important to people today?

The Bible message is a gift to us from God. It is also a gift to us from many people. It took many years and many people to give us this gift! As we read our Bibles, we learn more about God's great love for all people and how Jesus taught us to live. The

2 Peter

Now turn again to the NEW Testament list of books.

In the New Testament list, you will see that more than one book has the word "John" in its name, but they are not all together in the list.

How many books in the New Testament have the word "John" in their name? _______________

131

bottom

132

The little notes at the bottom of the page that give more information are called ____________________.

Four

(Look until you find all four.)

Find the book JOHN in your Bible.

It is in the New Testament list.

BE CAREFUL!
FIND JOHN
NOT 1 JOHN
(FIRST JOHN).

bottom

footnote

FOOTNOTES are little notes that give you more information.

Footnotes are found at the ________________ of the page.

I GUESS THAT'S
WHY THEY'RE
CALLED FOOTNOTES!

Now find the book 1 JOHN.

Do we say:

______ First John

or

______ 1 (One) John?

129

gospel

130

When you see a little letter (like *a*, *b*, *h*, or *m*) by a word as you read in the Bible, you know it tells you to look at the _____(top) or _____ (bottom) of the page.

There you will find a f__________.

Ḟirst

Find the book 2 JOHN.

REMEMBER,
WE SAY,
"SECOND JOHN."
IT COMES RIGHT
AFTER 1 JOHN.

<u>footnote</u>

Look up MARK 1:1 in your Bible. This little ***a*** in verse 1 means "look for FOOTNOTE ***a***."

Now see if you can find footnote ***a*** at the bottom of the page. Footnote ***a*** tells more about verse 1.

Footnote ***a*** says:

"Or ________________."

You know that 1 JOHN and 2 JOHN are not the same book.

The NUMBER at the front of the book helps you know which book you want.

When two or more books in the Bible have almost the same name, you can tell them apart by the n ___ ___ ___ ___ ___.

LET'S REST!
(AFTER YOU CHECK YOUR ANSWER.)
REMEMBER YOUR BOOKMARK.

First

12

second

31

14

first 1

Now, let's learn about small letters ***a, b,*** that mean something else.

Here is a picture of the beginning of the Gospel of Mark. There is a small ***a*** and ***b*** on this page.

These little letters mean "look at the BOTTOM of the page" for a footnote if you want to learn more.

At the bottom of the page is another small ***a*** with more information about certain words in verse 1.

This extra information at the bottom of the page is called a

___ ___ ___ ___ ___ ___ ___ ___.

1153 **Mark 1**

The Proclamation of John the Baptist

1 The beginning of the good news[a] of Jesus Christ, the Son of God.[b]
2 As it is written in the prophet Ī·sāi·ah,[c]
"See, I am sending my messenger ahead of you,[d]
who will prepare your way;
3 the voice of one crying out in the wilderness:
'Prepare the way of the Lord,
make his paths straight,' "
4 John the baptizer appeared[e] in the wilderness, proclaiming a baptism of repentance for the forgiveness of sins. 5 And people from the whole Judean countryside and all the people of Jerusalem were going out to him, and were baptized by him in the river Jordan, confessing their sins. 6 Now John was clothed with camel's hair, with a leather belt around his waist, and he ate locusts and wild honey. 7 He proclaimed, "The one who is more powerful than I is coming after me; I am not worthy to stoop down and untie the thong of his sandals. 8 I have baptized you with[f] water; but he will baptize you with[f] the Holy Spirit."

The Baptism of Jesus

9 In those days Jesus came from Nazareth of Galilee and was baptized by John in the Jordan. 10 And just as he was coming up out of the water, he saw the heavens torn apart and the Spirit descending like a dove on him. 11 And a voice came from heaven, "You are my Son, the Beloved;[g] with you I am well pleased."

When people came to John to be baptized, he told them that someone else would come after him. He said that he did not deserve to untie the sandals of the one coming. John was talking about the coming of Jesus, and he was saying that he did not deserve even to be a servant to Jesus. Later in his ministry, Jesus himself would wash the disciples' feet (see John 13:1–20). In this way, Jesus showed that those who follow God must always be looking for ways to serve other people.

The Temptation of Jesus

12 And the Spirit immediately drove him out into the wilderness. 13 He was in the wilderness forty days, tempted by Satan; and he was with the wild beasts, and the angels waited on him.

The Beginning of the Galilean Ministry

14 Now after John was arrested, Jesus came to Galilee, proclaiming the good news[a] of God,[h] 15 and saying, "The time is fulfilled, and the kingdom of God has come near;[i] repent, and believe in the good news."[a]

The first people Jesus called to be his followers were fishermen on the Sea of Galilee, a heart-shaped, inland lake that empties into the Jordan River.

Jesus Calls the First Disciples

16 As Jesus passed along the Sea of Galilee, he saw Simon and his brother Andrew casting a net into the sea—for they were fishermen. 17 And Jesus said to them, "Follow me and I will make you fish for people." 18 And immediately they left their nets and followed him. 19 As he went a little farther, he saw James son of Zeb'e·dee and his brother John, who were in their boat mending the nets. 20 Immediately he called them; and they left their father Zeb'e·dee in the boat with the hired men, and followed him.

[a] Or *gospel* [b] Other ancient authorities lack *the Son of God* [c] Other ancient authorities read *in the prophets* [d] Gk *before your face* [e] Other ancient authorities read *John was baptizing* [f] Or *in* [g] Or *my beloved Son* [h] Other ancient authorities read *of the kingdom* [i] Or *is at hand*

number

In many Bibles, there is a dictionary in the Bible. Often the dictionaries are in the back of the Bible.

Does your Bible have a dictionary?

Is it in the front or the back of your Bible?

See if you can find the words "Jesus Christ" in your dictionary. Can you read what it says about Jesus Christ out loud?

Who

glory

The reference:

1 CORINTHIANS 12:31b through 14:1a

means that you find ________________ Corinthians, Chapter

________________.

You begin reading there at the ________________ part of verse

__________ and read to the end of Chapter 13.

Then you read on into Chapter __________ to the end of the

________________ part of verse __________.

THAT WAS A LOT OF WORK, WASN'T IT? CHECK YOUR ANSWERS ON THE NEXT PAGE AND THEN STOP AND TAKE A REST. YOU DESERVE IT!

Now you know how to find any book in the Bible.

You are ready to learn how to find any part of any book in the Bible.

A Bible REFERENCE (pronounced REF er ens) tells you where to look to find a part of a book in the Bible.

If your teacher says, "Look up John three sixteen," she or he is giving you a Bible r e f e r ___ ___ ___ ___.

God

made

Look up PSALM 24:8a in your Bible.

Write the first word of Psalm 24:8a here: ___________

Write the last word of Psalm 24:8a here:

____________________.

(Did you look up the FIRST part of PSALM 24:8?)

reference

Your teacher would WRITE the reference like this:

JOHN 3:16

(She would SAY, “John three, sixteen.”)

The first thing a Bible reference tells you is which BOOK in the Bible you are to look up.

In the reference JOHN 3:16, the word “John” is the name of the ________________ you are to find.

first

Look up PSALM 100:3a, b in your Bible.

It says,

"Know that the LORD is ________________.

It is he that ________________ us, and we are his;"

(This Bible reference tells you to read ONLY the first and second parts of verse 3, even though the verse has three parts.)

book

This is a picture of the beginning of the Book of John. The big number 1 means "Chapter 1 begins here."

The Word Became Flesh

1 In the beginning was the Word,
and the Word was with God, and
the Word was God. 2He was in the
beginning with God. 3All things came
into being through him, and without
him not one thing came into being.
What has come into being 4in him was
life,[a] and the life was the light of all people. 5The light shines in the darkness,
and the darkness did not overcome it.
6 There was a man sent from God,
whose name was John. 7He came as a witness to testify to the light, so that all might
believe through him. 8He himself was not
the light, but he came to testify to the
light. 9The true light, which enlightens
everyone, was coming into the world.[b]
10 He was in the world, and the world
came into being through him; yet the world
did not know him. 11He came to what was
his own,[c] and his own people did not
accept him. 12But to all who received him,
who believed in his name, he gave power
to become children of God, 13who were
born, not of blood or of the will of the flesh
or of the will of man, but of God.
14 And the Word became flesh and
lived among us, and we have seen his
glory, the glory as of a father's only son,[d]
full of grace and truth. 15(John testified to
him and cried out, "This was he of whom
I said, 'He who comes after me ranks
ahead of me because he was before me.' ")
16From his fullness we have all received,
grace upon grace. 17The law indeed was
given through Moses; grace and truth
came through Jesus Christ. 18No one has
ever seen God. It is God the only Son,[e]
who is close to the Father's heart,[f] who has
made him known.

The Testimony of John the Baptist

19 This is the testimony given by John
when the Jews sent priests and Lē′vītes
from Jerusalem to ask him, "Who are
you?" 20He confessed and did not deny it,
but confessed, "I am not the Messiah."[g]
21And they asked him, "What then? Are

Have you ever thought about how many light bulbs it takes to light a house? Walk through your home, and count how many light bulbs there are! Think about how dark it would be at night without those lights.

John called Jesus "the light of the world." Jesus often told stories that had to do with light. Read Matthew 5:14–16, Matthew 6:22–23, and Luke 8:16–18. What do you think "light" stands for in each passage? Thank God for sending Jesus to be the light for our world.

you E·lī′jah?" He said, "I am not." "Are
you the prophet?" He answered, "No."
22Then they said to him, "Who are you?
Let us have an answer for those who sent
us. What do you say about yourself?" 23He
said,

"I am the voice of one crying out in the
wilderness,
'Make straight the way of the Lord,' "

as the prophet Ī·sāi′ah said.
24 Now they had been sent from the
Phar′i·sees. 25They asked him, "Why then
are you baptizing if you are neither the
Messiah,[g] nor E·lī′jah, nor the prophet?"
26John answered them, "I baptize with
water. Among you stands one whom you
do not know, 27the one who is coming
after me; I am not worthy to untie the
thong of his sandal." 28This took place in
Beth′a·ny across the Jordan where John
was baptizing.

The Lamb of God

29 The next day he saw Jesus coming
toward him and declared, "Here is the
Lamb of God who takes away the sin of

[a] Or 3*through him. And without him not one thing came into being that has come into being.* 4*In him was life* [b] Or *He was the true light that enlightens everyone coming into the world* [c] Or *to his own home* [d] Or *the Father's only Son* [e] Other ancient authorities read *It is an only Son, God,* or *It is the only Son* [f] Gk *bosom* [g] Or *the Christ*

Circle the big number 1 in this picture.

123

second

124

If you were told, "Keep on reading through verse 8a," that would mean you would stop after reading the ________________ part of verse 8.

The Word Became Flesh

In the beginning was the Word, and the Word was with God, and the Word was God. 2 He was in the beginning with God. 3 All things came into being through him, and without him not one thing came into being. What has come into being 4 in him was life,[a] and the life was the light of all people. 5 The light shines in the darkness, and the darkness did not overcome it.

6 There was a man sent from God, whose name was John. 7 He came as a witness to testify to the light, so that all might believe through him. 8 He himself was not the light, but he came to testify to the light. 9 The true light, which enlightens everyone, was coming into the world.[b]

10 He was in the world, and the world came into being through him; yet the world did not know him. 11 He came to what was his own,[c] and his own people did not accept him. 12 But to all who received him, who believed in his name, he gave power to become children of God, 13 who were born, not of blood or of the will of the flesh or of the will of man, but of God.

14 And the Word became flesh and lived among us, and we have seen his glory, the glory as of a father's only son,[d] full of grace and truth. 15 (John testified to him and cried out, "This was he of whom I said, 'He who comes after me ranks ahead of me because he was before me.'") 16 From his fullness we have all received, grace upon grace. 17 The law indeed was given through Moses; grace and truth came through Jesus Christ. 18 No one has ever seen God. It is God the only Son,[e] who is close to the Father's heart,[f] who has made him known.

The Testimony of John the Baptist

19 This is the testimony given by John when the Jews sent priests and Levites from Jerusalem to ask him, "Who are you?" 20 He confessed and did not deny it, but confessed, "I am not the Messiah."[g] 21 And they asked him, "What then? Are you Elijah?" He said, "I am not." "Are you the prophet?" He answered, "No." 22 Then they said to him, "Who are you? Let us have an answer for those who sent us. What do you say about yourself?" 23 He said,

"I am the voice of one crying out in the wilderness,
'Make straight the way of the Lord,'"
as the prophet Isaiah said.

24 Now they had been sent from the Pharisees. 25 They asked him, "Why then are you baptizing if you are neither the Messiah,[g] nor Elijah, nor the prophet?" 26 John answered them, "I baptize with water. Among you stands one whom you do not know, 27 the one who is coming after me; I am not worthy to untie the thong of his sandal." 28 This took place in Bethany across the Jordan where John was baptizing.

The Lamb of God

29 The next day he saw Jesus coming toward him and declared, "Here is the Lamb of God who takes away the sin of

Have you ever thought about how many light bulbs it takes to light a house? Walk through your home, and count how many light bulbs there are! Think about how dark it would be at night without those lights.

John called Jesus "the light of the world." Jesus often told stories that had to do with light. Read Matthew 5:14-16, Matthew 6:22-23, and Luke 8:16-18. What do you think "light" stands for in each passage? Thank God for sending Jesus to be the light for our world.

[a] Or through him. And without him not one thing came into being that has come into being. In him was life [b] Or He was the true light that enlightens everyone coming into the world [c] Or to his own home [d] Or the Father's only Son [e] Other ancient authorities read It is an only Son, God, or It is the only Son [f] Gk bosom [g] Or the Christ

Most of the books of the Bible have been divided into large parts called CHAPTERS.

The beginning of each ________________ is marked with a BIG number.

122

first

123

In a Bible reference like PSALM 33:5b, the “b” after the “5” means that you read the ________________ part of verse 5.

chapter

The beginning of the FIRST CHAPTER of a book in the Bible is marked with a big number __________.

Psalm 100

All Lands Summoned to Praise God

A Psalm of thanksgiving.

1 Make a joyful noise to the LORD, all the
earth.
2 Worship the LORD with gladness;
come into his presence with singing.

3 Know that the LORD is God.
It is he that made us, and we are his;[q]
we are his people, and the sheep of
his pasture.

4 Enter his gates with thanksgiving,
and his courts with praise.
Give thanks to him, bless his name.

5 For the LORD is good;
his steadfast love endures forever,
and his faithfulness to all
generations.

In the Bible reference: MATTHEW 28:19a

the "a" after the "19" means that you read only the

________________ part of verse 19.

1

The big number 1 shows you where

C ___ ___ ___ ___ ___ ___ 1 begins.

Psalm 100

All Lands Summoned to Praise God

A Psalm of thanksgiving.

1 Make a joyful noise to the LORD, all the
earth.
2 Worship the LORD with gladness;
come into his presence with singing.

3 Know that the LORD is God.
It is he that made us, and we are his;[q]
we are his people, and the sheep of
his pasture.

4 Enter his gates with thanksgiving,
and his courts with praise.
Give thanks to him, bless his name.

5 For the LORD is good;
his steadfast love endures forever,
and his faithfulness to all
generations.

In this picture, draw a circle around all the words of PSALM 100:5a.

BE SURE YOU CIRCLE ONLY VERSE 5, PART a.

Psalm 100

All Lands Summoned to Praise God

A Psalm of thanksgiving.

1 Make a joyful noise to the LORD, all the
earth.
2 Worship the LORD with gladness;
come into his presence with singing.

3 Know that the LORD is God.
It is he that made us, and we are his;[q]
we are his people, and the sheep of
his pasture.

4 Enter his gates with thanksgiving,
and his courts with praise.
Give thanks to him, bless his name.

5 For the LORD is good;
his steadfast love endures forever,
and his faithfulness to all
generations.

Chapter

In a Bible reference, the first number AFTER the name of the book tells you which chapter to look in.

In the reference JOHN 1, the number 1 comes AFTER the name of the book and tells you to look in the first ________________ of the Book of John.

b

Here is a picture of the beginning of PSALM 100.

Psalm 100:2a says, "Worship the LORD with gladness;".

Psalm 100:3b says, "It is he that made us, and we are his;".

Draw a circle around all the words of PSALM 100:3c in the picture.

Psalm 100

All Lands Summoned to Praise God

A Psalm of thanksgiving.

1 Make a joyful noise to the LORD, all the earth.
2 Worship the LORD with gladness;
come into his presence with singing.

3 Know that the LORD is God.
It is he that made us, and we are his;[q]
we are his people, and the sheep of his pasture.

4 Enter his gates with thanksgiving,
and his courts with praise.
Give thanks to him, bless his name.

5 For the LORD is good;
his steadfast love endures forever,
and his faithfulness to all generations.

REMEMBER! YOU ARE LOOKING FOR VERSE 3, AND PART C IS THE THIRD PART OF THE VERSE.

Chapter

In a Bible reference, you know which CHAPTER you are to find by: the first number _______ (before)

or

by: the first number _______ (after)

the name of the book.

(Check the right word [before or after]).

118

first

119

In Bible references, the FIRST part of a verse is called “a.”

The SECOND part of a verse is called “__________.”

The THIRD part of a verse is called “c.”

after

REMEMBER!
1 JOHN MEANS
THE BOOK,
FIRST JOHN.
JOHN 1 MEANS
THE BOOK JOHN,
CHAPTER 1.

We write FIRST JOHN this way:

_____ John 1

or

_____ 1 John

a

The letter a means "the FIRST part of a verse."

The letter b means "the SECOND part of a verse."

The letter c means "the THIRD part of a verse."

In the Bible reference: PSALM 100:2a (say "Salm")

the letter a after the number 2 means that you read only the

________________ part of verse 2.

1 John

The Bible reference JOHN 1 means:

_____ the Book of John, Chapter 1

_____ First John

1 1

7 15

Sometimes you will be given a reference that tells you to look up only a PART OF A VERSE.

In the Bible reference: PSALM 100:2a

the letter **a** after the number 2 means that you read only the FIRST PART of verse 2.

In the Bible reference, Psalm 100:2a, the letter __________ means that you read only the FIRST PART OF VERSE 2.

****

NOTE: You SAY Psalms when you are talking about the whole Book of Psalms. You SAY Psalm when you are talking about one Psalm.

IN THE WORD, "PSALM," DON'T SAY THE "P." JUST SAY "SALM."

The Book of John,

Chapter 1

Now turn again in your Bible to the beginning of the Book of John in the New Testament.

Find the BIG number 2 in the Book of John. You may have to turn the page to find it. This is Chapter 2. (You would write it JOHN 2.)

The first words of Chapter 2 in the Book of John are:
"On the third ________________ . . . ."
(Fill in the missing word.)

read

skip

read

Sometimes you read verses in more than one chapter in the same book.

A semicolon (;) is used between each set of chapter and verse numbers.

In the Bible reference AMOS 1:1; 7:15,

(SAY, "Amos one, one, and seven, fifteen.")

first you read chapter __________, verse __________, and then you skip to chapter __________, verse __________ in the Book of Amos.

day

The big number 2 means _________________________ 2 begins here.

14 17

Sometimes you read different groups of verses in one chapter. A comma is also used here between the groups of verses. The comma (,) tells you which verses to skip.

In the reference: 1 JOHN 4:7-8, 11-13, you

_____ skip verses 7-8

_____ read verses 7-8

_____ skip verses 9-10

_____ read verses 9-10

_____ skip verses 11-13

_____ read verses 11-13

Chapter

Now find the big number 3 in the Book of John. It may be on the same page as Chapter 2.

The big number 3 shows you where Chapter 3 begins.

The first words of JOHN 3 are: "Now there was a

____________________ . . . ."

BE SURE YOU FIND THE BIG NUMBERS.

child

strong

Jesus

Just for fun, look up in your Bible a very important saying of Jesus to his friends.

JOHN 15:14, 17

You will read verses __________ and __________.

59

Pharisee

NOW, LET'S SEE IF YOU REMEMBER!

JOHN 2 means: _____ Second John or

_____ Book of John, Chapter 2

3 JOHN means: _____ Third John or

_____ Book of John, Chapter 3

JOHN 3 means: _____ Third John or

_____ Book of John, Chapter 3

(Check the THREE right answers.)

skip

Look up LUKE 2:40, 52 in your Bible.

Fill in the missing words in the verses below:

VERSE 40:

"The ________________ grew and became ______________________, filled with wisdom; and the favor of God was upon him."

VERSE 52:

"And _________________ increased in wisdom and in years, and in divine and human favor."

Book of John, Chapter 2

Third John

Book of John, Chapter 3

The Ten Commandments are found in the Bible in the Book of Exodus, Chapter 20.

Find EXODUS in your Bible.

Turn to the Book of Exodus and begin looking for the big number 20 that tells you where Chapter 20 begins.

It will help you to find the big "20" if you look at the numbers at the top of each page in your Bible.

The numbers at the top of the page show you which chapters are found on those pages.

EXODUS 20 begins: "Then ____________________ spoke . . . ."

52

In the Bible reference:

LUKE 2:40, 52

the comma (,) between the verse numbers means that you

_____ read all the verses between verse 40 and verse 52.

_____ skip all the verses between verse 40 and verse 52.

Check the right word.

God

The Ten Commandments are also found in the Bible in DEUTERONOMY 5.

Find the fifth chapter of Deuteronomy in your Bible.

Look until you have found the big number 5.

DEUTERONOMY 5 begins: "_________________ convened all Israel . . . ."

21

37

22

1

O. K. WE'VE HAD A REST- LET'S GO!

NOTICE THE COMMA.
NOW THAT IS
DIFFERENT!

Here is a tricky kind of Bible reference.

Look at it carefully.

LUKE 2:40, 52

(We SAY, "Luke two, forty AND fifty-two.")

The verse numbers in the reference are separated by a (,) instead of a hyphen (-).

When you look up this Bible reference, you read ONLY verse 40 AND verse ________________.

You skip all the verses in between.

Moses

Let's check one more time:

3 JOHN means: _____ Book of John, Chapter 3 or

_____ Third John

EXODUS 5 means: _____ Book of Exodus, Chapter 5 or

_____ Fifth Exodus

1 CORINTHIANS means: _____ Book of Corinthians, Chapter 1 or

_____ First Corinthians

LET'S REST! CHECK YOUR ANSWERS AND TAKE A REST.

all

The Bible reference:

LUKE 21:37 through 22:1

means that you are to find the Book of Luke, Chapter __________,

and begin reading at verse __________.

When you finish that chapter, you keep on reading in Chapter __________ to the end of verse __________.

HOW ABOUT A REST?
CHECK YOUR ANSWERS.
REMEMBER YOUR
BOOKMARK.

Third John

Book of Exodus, Chapter 5

First Corinthians

HERE WE GO AGAIN!

This is a picture of the beginning of Chapter 1 of the Book of Genesis.

The part that is circled is called a VERSE. The circled words are VERSE 1.

The little “2” tells you where VERSE 2 begins.

The little “3” tells you where ___ ___ ___ ___ ___ 3 begins.

Genesis 1 2

We call the book of Genesis by its Greek name, which means “beginning.” The opening words of the book of Genesis tell us that God is the creator and that in the beginning, God already existed.

Six Days of Creation and the Sabbath

1 In the beginning when God created[a]
the heavens and the earth, [2]the
earth was a formless void and darkness
covered the face of the deep, while a
wind from God[b] swept over the face of
the waters. [3]Then God said, “Let there be
light”; and there was light. [4]And God saw
that the light was good; and God separated the light from the darkness. [5]God
called the light Day, and the darkness he
called Night. And there was evening and
there was morning, the first day.
6 And God said, “Let there be a dome
in the midst of the waters, and let it separate the waters from the waters.” [7]So
God made the dome and separated the
waters that were under the dome from
the waters that were above the dome.
And it was so. [8]God called the dome Sky.
And there was evening and there was
morning, the second day.
9 And God said, “Let the waters
under the sky be gathered together into
one place, and let the dry land appear.”
And it was so. [10]God called the dry land
Earth, and the waters that were gathered
together he called Seas. And God saw
that it was good. [11]Then God said, “Let
the earth put forth vegetation: plants
yielding seed, and fruit trees of every
kind on earth that bear fruit with the
seed in it.” And it was so. [12]The earth
brought forth vegetation: plants yielding
seed of every kind, and trees of every
kind bearing fruit with the seed in it.
And God saw that it was good. [13]And
there was evening and there was morning, the third day.
14 And God said, “Let there be lights
in the dome of the sky to separate the day
from the night; and let them be for signs
and for seasons and for days and years,
[15]and let them be lights in the dome of
the sky to give light upon the earth.”
And it was so. [16]God made the two great
lights—the greater light to rule the day
and the lesser light to rule the night—and
the stars. [17]God set them in the dome of
the sky to give light upon the earth, [18]to
rule over the day and over the night, and
to separate the light from the darkness.
And God saw that it was good. [19]And
there was evening and there was morning, the fourth day.
20 And God said, “Let the waters
bring forth swarms of living creatures,
and let birds fly above the earth across the
dome of the sky.” [21]So God created the
great sea monsters and every living crea-
ture that moves, of every kind, with
which the waters swarm, and every
winged bird of every kind. And God saw
that it was good. [22]God blessed them, saying, “Be fruitful and multiply and fill the
waters in the seas, and let birds multiply
on the earth.” [23]And there was evening
and there was morning, the fifth day.
24 And God said, “Let the earth bring
forth living creatures of every kind: cat-
tle and creeping things and wild animals
of the earth of every kind.” And it was
so. [25]God made the wild animals of the

The more we learn about nature, the universe, or human beings, the more we are amazed by the miracle of God’s creation. Because God said, “Let there be light, sky, seas, dry land, plants, sun, moon, stars, fish, birds, animals, and people,” we have an awesome world!

[a] *Or when God began to create or In the beginning God created* [b] *Or while the spirit of God or while a mighty wind*

108

all

In a Bible reference, a hyphen is a short line between verse numbers. The word "through" tells you to go on reading into another chapter.

Both the hyphen and the word "through" tell you to read

_____ none of the verses between the numbers.

or

_____ all of the verses between the numbers.

verse

To make it easier to find things in the Bible, the CHAPTERS have been divided into small parts called VERSES.

In the picture of the beginning of the Book of Genesis, draw a circle around ALL the words in VERSE 5.

Six Days of Creation and the Sabbath

1 In the beginning when God created[a]
the heavens and the earth, [2]the
earth was a formless void and darkness
covered the face of the deep, while a
wind from God[b] swept over the face of
the waters. [3]Then God said, "Let there be
light"; and there was light. [4]And God saw
that the light was good; and God separated the light from the darkness. [5]God
called the light Day, and the darkness he
called Night. And there was evening and
there was morning, the first day.
6 And God said, "Let there be a dome
in the midst of the waters, and let it separate the waters from the waters."

1	18
2	12

NOTICE THE WORD "THROUGH"!

In the Bible reference MATTHEW 1:18 THROUGH 2:12

the word "through" means that you read

_____ none

_____ all

of the verses between Matthew 1:18 and Matthew 2:12.

Six Days of Creation and the Sabbath

1 In the beginning when God created[a]
the heavens and the earth, [2]the
earth was a formless void and darkness
covered the face of the deep, while a
wind from God[b] swept over the face of
the waters. [3]Then God said, "Let there be
light"; and there was light. [4]And God saw
that the light was good; and God separated the light from the darkness. [5]God
called the light Day, and the darkness he
called Night. And there was evening and
there was morning, the first day.

6 And God said, "Let there be a dome
in the midst of the waters, and let it separate the waters from the waters."

The books of the Bible have been divided into large parts called chapters.

Each of the CHAPTERS has been divided into small parts called V _______________.

25 37

all

Sometimes a story begins in one chapter and ends in a following chapter.

The Christmas story in Matthew begins at MATTHEW 1:18. It ends at MATTHEW 2:12.

Here is the way the Bible reference is written:

MATTHEW 1:18 through 2:12

You say, "Matthew one, eighteen through two, twelve."

This Bible reference means that you find the Book of Matthew, Chapter _____, and begin reading at verse __________. You keep on reading to the end of that chapter. You read on in the next chapter (Chapter __________) until you finish verse __________.

verses

This picture shows the beginning of Chapter 1 of the Book of Genesis in your Bible.

The BIG number tells where the ________________ begins.

The LITTLE numbers help us know where each VERSE begins.

Genesis 1 2

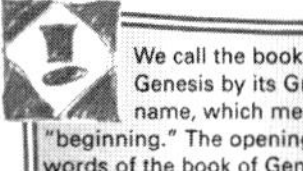

We call the book of Genesis by its Greek name, which means "beginning." The opening words of the book of Genesis tell us that God is the creator and that in the beginning, God already existed.

Six Days of Creation and the Sabbath

1 In the beginning when God created[a]
the heavens and the earth, [2]the
earth was a formless void and darkness
covered the face of the deep, while a
wind from God[b] swept over the face of
the waters. [3]Then God said, "Let there be
light"; and there was light. [4]And God saw
that the light was good; and God separated the light from the darkness. [5]God
called the light Day, and the darkness he
called Night. And there was evening and
there was morning, the first day.
6 And God said, "Let there be a dome
in the midst of the waters, and let it separate the waters from the waters." [7]So
God made the dome and separated the
waters that were under the dome from
the waters that were above the dome.
And it was so. [8]God called the dome Sky.
And there was evening and there was
morning, the second day.
9 And God said, "Let the waters
under the sky be gathered together into
one place, and let the dry land appear."
And it was so. [10]God called the dry land
Earth, and the waters that were gathered
together he called Seas. And God saw
that it was good. [11]Then God said, "Let
the earth put forth vegetation: plants
yielding seed, and fruit trees of every
kind on earth that bear fruit with the
seed in it." And it was so. [12]The earth
brought forth vegetation: plants yielding
seed of every kind, and trees of every
kind bearing fruit with the seed in it.
And God saw that it was good. [13]And
there was evening and there was morning, the third day.
14 And God said, "Let there be lights
in the dome of the sky to separate the day
from the night; and let them be for signs
and for seasons and for days and years,
[15]and let them be lights in the dome of
the sky to give light upon the earth."
And it was so. [16]God made the two great
lights—the greater light to rule the day
and the lesser light to rule the night—and
the stars. [17]God set them in the dome of
the sky to give light upon the earth, [18]to
rule over the day and over the night, and
to separate the light from the darkness.
And God saw that it was good. [19]And
there was evening and there was morning, the fourth day.
20 And God said, "Let the waters
bring forth swarms of living creatures,
and let birds fly above the earth across the
dome of the sky." [21]So God created the
great sea monsters and every living crea-
ture that moves, of every kind, with
which the waters swarm, and every
winged bird of every kind. And God saw
that it was good. [22]God blessed them, saying, "Be fruitful and multiply and fill the
waters in the seas, and let birds multiply
on the earth." [23]And there was evening
and there was morning, the fifth day.
24 And God said, "Let the earth bring
forth living creatures of every kind: cat-
tle and creeping things and wild animals
of the earth of every kind." And it was
so. [25]God made the wild animals of the

The more we learn about nature, the universe, or human beings, the more we are amazed by the miracle of God's creation. Because God said, "Let there be light, sky, seas, dry land, plants, sun, moon, stars, fish, birds, animals, and people," we have an awesome world!

[a] *Or when God began to create or In the beginning God created* [b] *Or while the spirit of God or while a mighty wind*

If you looked up Luke 10:25-37, you found that the story of the Good Samaritan begins, "Just then a lawyer stood up . . . ."

This story ends, "Jesus said to him, 'Go and do likewise.'"

There are lots of good stories in the Bible.

In the Bible reference:

LUKE 10:25-37,

you read from the beginning of verse __________ to the end of verse __________.

The hyphen (-) means that you read

_____ (all) of the verses between 25 and 37.

or

_____ (none) of the verses between 25 and 37.

(Check the right word.)

chapter

In the books of the Bible the BIG numbers tell us where the

___ ___ ___ ___ ___ ___ ___ s

begin.

The LITTLE numbers tell us where the ___ ___ ___ ___ ___ s begin.

1 In the beginning when God created[a]
the heavens and the earth, 2the
earth was a formless void and darkness
covered the face of the deep, while a
wind from God[b] swept over the face of
the waters. 3Then God said, "Let there be
light"; and there was light. 4And God saw
that the light was good; and God separated the light from the darkness. 5God
called the light Day, and the darkness he
called Night. And there was evening and
there was morning, the first day.

LORD

God

If you would like, you can find a story that Jesus told. The story is called "The Good Samaritan."

The Bible reference is LUKE 10:25-37.

When you are finished reading this parable or story, turn to the next page.

chapters

verses

To make it easier to find a place in a book in the Bible, most of the BOOKS of the Bible have been divided into large parts called

____________________________.

Blessed

Jesus studied the laws and rules of the Hebrew people in the Old Testament.

Find the most important rule of all:

DEUTERONOMY 6:4-5

Read the verses and write the missing words here:

"Hear, O Israel: The ________________ is our ________________, the LORD alone. You shall love the LORD your God with all your heart, and with all your soul, and with all your might."

chapters

These chapters have been divided into smaller parts called

____________________.

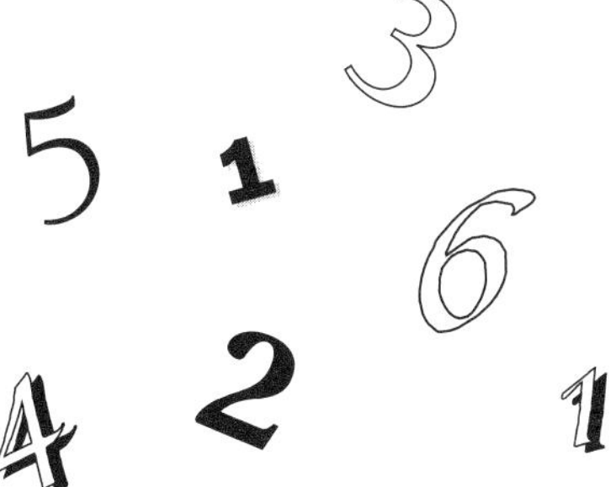

Luke

2

went

heart

Look in the Book of Matthew for some of Jesus' most famous teachings. Find: MATTHEW 5:3-12

Look at these verses in your Bible.

Almost every verse begins with the same word. Write that word in this blank: ______________________

THIS LIST
OF TEACHINGS
IS CALLED
"THE BEATITUDES."

verses

We can find any CHAPTER we are looking for because each chapter has been given a: _____ little number.

or a

_____ big number.

The Word Became Flesh

1 In the beginning was the Word,
and the Word was with God, and
the Word was God. 2He was in the
beginning with God. 3All things came
into being through him, and without
him not one thing came into being.
What has come into being 4in him was
life,[a] and the life was the light of all people. 5The light shines in the darkness,
and the darkness did not overcome it.
6 There was a man sent from God,
whose name was John. 7He came as a witness to testify to the light, so that all might
believe through him. 8He himself was not
the light, but he came to testify to the
light. 9The true light, which enlightens
everyone, was coming into the world.[b]

Now see if you can find the story about Jesus going on a trip when he was twelve years old.

The Bible reference is LUKE 2:41-51.

First, find the Book of ______________, Chapter __________. After you find the big number 2, be sure you look DOWN the page and in the next column, or on the next page until you find verse 41. (Depending on your version of the Bible, you may have to search to find verse 41.)

Verse 41 begins, "Now every year his parents __________ to Jerusalem. . . ."

Verse 51 ENDS with these words, "His mother treasured all these things in her ______________."

big

We can find any Bible VERSE we are looking for, because each verse has been given a:

_____ little number

or a

_____ big number.

The Word Became Flesh

1 In the beginning was the Word,
and the Word was with God, and
the Word was God. 2He was in the
beginning with God. 3All things came
into being through him, and without
him not one thing came into being.
What has come into being 4in him was
life,[a] and the life was the light of all people. 5The light shines in the darkness,
and the darkness did not overcome it.
6 There was a man sent from God,
whose name was John. 7He came as a witness to testify to the light, so that all might
believe through him. 8He himself was not
the light, but he came to testify to the
light. 9The true light, which enlightens
everyone, was coming into the world.[b]

Suppose your teacher gives you the Bible reference:

JOHN 1:6-7

(John one, six through seven)

On this picture, draw a line around verses 6 through 7.

Check again to see that you marked only two verses for reading!

little

Check the right word.

The chapter numbers are:

_____ larger

or

_____ smaller

than the verse numbers.

In this picture of the first part of the Book of John, DRAW A CIRCLE around the CHAPTER number.

John 1 1226

The Word Became Flesh

1 In the beginning was the Word,
and the Word was with God, and
the Word was God. 2 He was in the
beginning with God. 3 All things came
into being through him, and without
him not one thing came into being.
What has come into being 4 in him was
life,[a] and the life was the light of all people. 5 The light shines in the darkness,
and the darkness did not overcome it.
6 There was a man sent from God,
whose name was John. 7 He came as a witness to testify to the light, so that all might
believe through him. 8 He himself was not
the light, but he came to testify to the
light. 9 The true light, which enlightens
everyone, was coming into the world.[b]
10 He was in the world, and the world
came into being through him; yet the world
did not know him. 11 He came to what was
his own,[c] and his own people did not
accept him. 12 But to all who received him,
who believed in his name, he gave power
to become children of God, 13 who were
born, not of blood or of the will of the flesh
or of the will of man, but of God.
14 And the Word became flesh and
lived among us, and we have seen his
glory, the glory as of a father's only son,[d]
full of grace and truth. 15 (John testified to
him and cried out, "This was he of whom
I said, 'He who comes after me ranks
ahead of me because he was before me.' ")
16 From his fullness we have all received,
grace upon grace. 17 The law indeed was
given through Moses; grace and truth
came through Jesus Christ. 18 No one has
ever seen God. It is God the only Son,[e]
who is close to the Father's heart,[f] who has
made him known.

The Testimony of John the Baptist

19 This is the testimony given by John
when the Jews sent priests and Lē´vītes
from Jerusalem to ask him, "Who are
you?" 20 He confessed and did not deny it,
but confessed, "I am not the Messiah."[g]
21 And they asked him, "What then? Are
you E·lī´jah?" He said, "I am not." "Are
you the prophet?" He answered, "No."
22 Then they said to him, "Who are you?
Let us have an answer for those who sent
us. What do you say about yourself?" 23 He
said,

"I am the voice of one crying out in the
wilderness,
'Make straight the way of the Lord,' "

as the prophet Ī·sāi´ah said.
24 Now they had been sent from the
Phar´i·sees. 25 They asked him, "Why then
are you baptizing if you are neither the
Messiah,[g] nor E·lī´jah, nor the prophet?"
26 John answered them, "I baptize with
water. Among you stands one whom you
do not know, 27 the one who is coming
after me; I am not worthy to untie the
thong of his sandal." 28 This took place in
Beth´a·ny across the Jordan where John
was baptizing.

The Lamb of God

29 The next day he saw Jesus coming
toward him and declared, "Here is the
Lamb of God who takes away the sin of

Have you ever thought about how many light bulbs it takes to light a house? Walk through your home, and count how many light bulbs there are! Think about how dark it would be at night without those lights.

John called Jesus "the light of the world." Jesus often told stories that had to do with light. Read Matthew 5:14–16, Matthew 6:22–23, and Luke 8:16–18. What do you think "light" stands for in each passage? Thank God for sending Jesus to be the light for our world.

[a] Or 3 *through him. And without him not one thing came into being that has come into being.* 4 *In him was life* [b] Or *He was the true light that enlightens everyone coming into the world* [c] Or *to his own home* [d] Or *the Father's only Son* [e] Other ancient authorities read *It is an only Son, God,* or *It is the only Son* [f] Gk *bosom* [g] Or *the Christ*

end

Here is a picture of the beginning of Chapter 1 of the Book of John.

Suppose your teacher gives you the Bible reference:

JOHN 1:1-5

(John one, one through five)

On this picture draw a line around verses 1 through 5.

The Word Became Flesh

1 In the beginning was the Word,
and the Word was with God, and
the Word was God. [2]He was in the
beginning with God. [3]All things came
into being through him, and without
him not one thing came into being.
What has come into being [4]in him was
life,[a] and the life was the light of all people. [5]The light shines in the darkness,
and the darkness did not overcome it.
6 There was a man sent from God,
whose name was John. [7]He came as a witness to testify to the light, so that all might
believe through him. [8]He himself was not
the light, but he came to testify to the
light. [9]The true light, which enlightens
everyone, was coming into the world.[b]

BE CAREFUL!
BE SURE YOU
INCLUDE ALL OF
VERSES 1-5.

larger

The Word Became Flesh

1 In the beginning was the Word, and the Word was with God, and the Word was God. 2He was in the beginning with God. 3All things came into being through him, and without him not one thing came into being. What has come into being 4in him was life,[a] and the life was the light of all people. 5The light shines in the darkness, and the darkness did not overcome it.

6 There was a man sent from God, whose name was John. 7He came as a witness to testify to the light, so that all might believe through him. 8He himself was not the light, but he came to testify to the light. 9The true light, which enlightens everyone, was coming into the world.[b]

10 He was in the world, and the world came into being through him; yet the world did not know him. 11He came to what was his own,[c] and his own people did not accept him. 12But to all who received him, who believed in his name, he gave power to become children of God, 13who were born, not of blood or of the will of the flesh or of the will of man, but of God.

14 And the Word became flesh and lived among us, and we have seen his glory, the glory as of a father's only son,[d] full of grace and truth. 15(John testified to him and cried out, "This was he of whom I said, 'He who comes after me ranks ahead of me because he was before me.'") 16From his fullness we have all received, grace upon grace. 17The law indeed was given through Moses; grace and truth came through Jesus Christ. 18No one has ever seen God. It is God the only Son,[e] who is close to the Father's heart,[f] who has made him known.

The Testimony of John the Baptist

19 This is the testimony given by John when the Jews sent priests and Levites from Jerusalem to ask him, "Who are you?" 20He confessed and did not deny it, but confessed, "I am not the Messiah."[g] 21And they asked him, "What then? Are

Have you ever thought about how many light bulbs it takes to light a house? Walk through your home, and count how many light bulbs there are! Think about how dark it would be at night without those lights.

John called Jesus "the light of the world." Jesus often told stories that had to do with light. Read Matthew 5:14-16, Matthew 6:22-23, and Luke 8:16-18. What do you think "light" stands for in each passage? Thank God for sending Jesus to be the light for our world.

you Elijah?" He said, "I am not." "Are you the prophet?" He answered, "No." 22Then they said to him, "Who are you? Let us have an answer for those who sent us. What do you say about yourself?" 23He said,

"I am the voice of one crying out in the wilderness,
'Make straight the way of the Lord,'"
as the prophet Isaiah said.

24 Now they had been sent from the Pharisees. 25They asked him, "Why then are you baptizing if you are neither the Messiah,[h] nor Elijah, nor the prophet?" 26John answered them, "I baptize with water. Among you stands one whom you do not know, 27the one who is coming after me; I am not worthy to untie the thong of his sandal." 28This took place in Bethany across the Jordan where John was baptizing.

The Lamb of God

29 The next day he saw Jesus coming toward him and declared, "Here is the Lamb of God who takes away the sin of

[a] Or through him. And without him not one thing came into being that has come into being. In him was life [b] Or He was the true light that enlightens everyone coming into the world [c] Or to his own home [d] Or the Father's only Son [e] Other ancient authorities read It is an only Son, God, or It is the only Son [f] Gk bosom [g] Or the Christ

The verse numbers are:

_____ larger or

_____ smaller

than the chapter numbers.

In this picture of the first part of the Book of John, draw a circle around EACH VERSE NUMBER. You should find EIGHT verse numbers in this picture.

The Word Became Flesh

1 In the beginning was the Word, and the Word was with God, and the Word was God. 2He was in the beginning with God. 3All things came into being through him, and without him not one thing came into being. What has come into being 4in him was life,[a] and the life was the light of all people. 5The light shines in the darkness, and the darkness did not overcome it.

6 There was a man sent from God, whose name was John. 7He came as a witness to testify to the light, so that all might believe through him. 8He himself was not the light, but he came to testify to the light. 9The true light, which enlightens everyone, was coming into the world.[b]

chapter

verse

verse

In the Bible reference

LUKE 2:1-20

you BEGIN reading at verse 1.

You STOP reading at the _____ (beginning) of verse 20.

or

the _____ (end) of verse 20.

(Check the right word.)

smaller

The Word Became Flesh

1 In the beginning was the Word,
and the Word was with God, and
the Word was God. 2He was in the
beginning with God. 3All things came
into being through him, and without
him not one thing came into being.
What has come into being 4in him was
life,[a] and the life was the light of all people. 5The light shines in the darkness,
and the darkness did not overcome it.
6 There was a man sent from God,
whose name was John. 7He came as a witness to testify to the light, so that all might
believe through him. 8He himself was not
the light, but he came to testify to the
light. 9The true light, which enlightens
everyone, was coming into the world.[b]

A verse number tells where a verse begins.

A verse ends when you come to the next verse number or when you come to the end of a section.

In this picture, all the words of verse 7 are circled.

Now circle all the words of verse 4 in this picture.

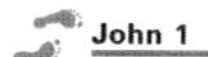

John 1

The Word Became Flesh

1 In the beginning was the Word,
and the Word was with God, and
the Word was God. 2He was in the
beginning with God. 3All things came
into being through him, and without
him not one thing came into being.
What has come into being 4in him was
life,[a] and the life was the light of all people. 5The light shines in the darkness,
and the darkness did not overcome it.
6 There was a man sent from God,
whose name was John. 7He came as a witness to testify to the light, so that all might
believe through him. 8He himself was not
the light, but he came to testify to the
light. 9The true light, which enlightens
everyone, was coming into the world.[b]
10 He was in the world, and the world
came into being through him; yet the world
did not know him. 11He came to what was
his own,[c] and his own people did not
accept him. 12But to all who received him,
who believed in his name, he gave power
to become children of God, 13who were
born, not of blood or of the will of the flesh
or of the will of man, but of God.
14 And the Word became flesh and
lived among us, and we have seen his
glory, the glory as of a father's only son,[d]
full of grace and truth. 15(John testified to
him and cried out, "This was he of whom
I said, 'He who comes after me ranks
ahead of me because he was before me.' ")
16From his fullness we have all received,
grace upon grace. 17The law indeed was
given through Moses; grace and truth
came through Jesus Christ. 18No one has
ever seen God. It is God the only Son,[e]
who is close to the Father's heart,[f] who has
made him known.

Have you ever thought about how many light bulbs it takes to light a house? Walk through your home, and count how many light bulbs there are! Think about how dark it would be at night without those lights.

John called Jesus "the light of the world." Jesus often told stories that had to do with light. Read Matthew 5:14–16, Matthew 6:22–23, and Luke 8:16–18. What do you think "light" stands for in each passage? Thank God for sending Jesus to be the light for our world.

The Testimony of John the Baptist

19 This is the testimony given by John
when the Jews sent priests and Lē′vītes
from Jerusalem to ask him, "Who are
you?" 20He confessed and did not deny it,
but confessed, "I am not the Messiah."[g]
21And they asked him, "What then? Are
you E·lī′jah?" He said, "I am not." "Are
you the prophet?" He answered, "No."
22Then they said to him, "Who are you?
Let us have an answer for those who sent
us. What do you say about yourself?" 23He
said,

"I am the voice of one crying out in the
wilderness,
'Make straight the way of the Lord,' "

as the prophet Ī·sāi′ah said.
24 Now they had been sent from the
Phar′i·sees. 25They asked him, "Why then
are you baptizing if you are neither the
Messiah,[g] nor E·lī′jah, nor the prophet?"
26John answered them, "I baptize with
water. Among you stands one whom you
do not know, 27the one who is coming
after me; I am not worthy to untie the
thong of his sandal." 28This took place in
Beth′a·ny across the Jordan where John
was baptizing.

The Lamb of God

29 The next day he saw Jesus coming
toward him and declared, "Here is the
Lamb of God who takes away the sin of

[a] Or *through him. And without him not one thing came into being that has come into being. In him was life* [b] Or *He was the true light that enlightens everyone coming into the world* [c] Or *to his own home* [d] Or *the Father's only Son* [e] Other ancient authorities read *It is an only Son, God,* or *It is the only Son* [f] Gk *bosom* [g] Or *the Christ*

1 20

Check the right words.

In the Bible reference LUKE 2:1-20

the number 2 is a _____ (chapter) number

or

a _____ (verse) number

the number 1 is a _____ (chapter) number

or

a _____ (verse) number

the number 20 is a _____ (chapter) number

or

a _____ (verse) number

The Word Became Flesh

1 In the beginning was the Word,
and the Word was with God, and
the Word was God. [2]He was in the
beginning with God. [3]All things came
into being through him, and without
him not one thing came into being.
What has come into being [4]in him was
life,[a] and the life was the light of all people. [5]The light shines in the darkness,
and the darkness did not overcome it.
6 There was a man sent from God,
whose name was John. [7]He came as a witness to testify to the light, so that all might
believe through him. [8]He himself was not
the light, but he came to testify to the
light. [9]The true light, which enlightens
everyone, was coming into the world.[b]

Sometimes in a Bible you will see a "Timeline." A Timeline tells you when certain events in the Bible happened. See if you have a Timeline in your Bible. Sometimes Timelines are found near the front of a Bible.

If you can locate a Timeline in your Bible, does it tell you the approximate year that Moses was born? ____________

Does your Timeline tell you the approximate time the Israelites entered the Promised Land? ______________

Notice that the numbers are larger and then get smaller as they get closer to the birth of Jesus. After the birth of Jesus, the numbers go up again.

Does your Timeline tell you when Pentecost was? __________

2 1

20

THIS LITTLE MARK IS CALLED
A HYPHEN (SAY, "HI FUN.")

In the Bible reference

LUKE 2:1-20

the hyphen (-) means that you READ ALL

THE VERSES from verse __________ through verse __________.

About 1350 B.C.

About 1200 B.C.

After 30 A.D.

Turn in your Bible to the Book of Genesis and find Chapter 1.

You will find the BIG number 1 for Chapter 1, but you will not find the LITTLE number 1 for verse 1.

The number for VERSE 1 is not printed in most Bibles.

Six Days of Creation and the Sabbath

1 In the beginning when God created[a] the heavens and the earth, [2]the earth was a formless void and darkness covered the face of the deep, while a wind from God[b] swept over the face of the waters. [3]Then God said, "Let there be light"; and there was light. [4]And God saw that the light was good; and God separated the light from the darkness. [5]God called the light Day, and the darkness he called Night. And there was evening and there was morning, the first day.

Do you think you can find the words of verse 1, even if the verse number is not printed there? _____ Yes _____ No

Matthew(1): [18]

But most of the time you will read more than one verse.

Suppose you see a reference like this:

LUKE 2:1-20

(SAY, "Luke two, one through twenty.")

This means that you are to find the Book of Luke, Chapter __________, and begin reading at verse ___________. You keep on reading ALL the verses on to the END of verse __________.

Yes

Now turn in your Bible to the Book of John in the New Testament.

In the Bible, every chapter begins with verse 1, even if the number is not printed there.

Circle ALL the words of verse 1 in this picture.

Be careful! Circle only the words of VERSE 1.

The Word Became Flesh

1 In the beginning was the Word,
and the Word was with God, and
the Word was God. [2]He was in the
beginning with God. [3]All things came
into being through him, and without
him not one thing came into being.
What has come into being [4]in him was
life,[a] and the life was the light of all people. [5]The light shines in the darkness,
and the darkness did not overcome it.
6 There was a man sent from God,
whose name was John. [7]He came as a witness to testify to the light, so that all might
believe through him. [8]He himself was not
the light, but he came to testify to the
light. [9]The true light, which enlightens
everyone, was coming into the world.[b]

1

18

In the Bible reference

MATTHEW 1:18

draw a square around the verse number.

draw a circle around the chapter number.

The Word Became Flesh

1 In the beginning was the Word,
and the Word was with God, and
the Word was God. [2]He was in the
beginning with God. [3]All things came
into being through him, and without
him not one thing came into being.
What has come into being [4]in him was
life,[a] and the life was the light of all people. [5]The light shines in the darkness,
and the darkness did not overcome it.
6 There was a man sent from God,
whose name was John. [7]He came as a witness to testify to the light, so that all might
believe through him. [8]He himself was not
the light, but he came to testify to the
light. [9]The true light, which enlightens
everyone, was coming into the world.[b]

THIS MARK : IS CALLED A ***COLON.***

In a Bible reference like John 3:16, the number after the name of the book is the CHAPTER number: John **3**:16

The number after the (:) is the VERSE number.

In the reference

JOHN **3**:16

the number 3 is the ______ verse number

or

the number 3 is the _____ chapter number.

Check the right word.

birth

IF YOU FOUND THE VERSE IN MATTHEW WITHOUT ANY TROUBLE, YOU ARE GETTING VERY GOOD AT LOOKING UP BIBLE REFERENCES!

In the Bible reference

MATTHEW 1:18

the chapter number is __________

the verse number is __________

chapter

In the reference

JOHN 3:16

the number 16 is the _____ verse number

or

the number 16 is the _____ chapter number.

days

Let us look up another Bible reference.

Not all of the Christmas story is found in Luke. Some of it begins with MATTHEW 1:18.

Find MATTHEW 1:18 in your Bible.

First, find the BIG number 1. Then look DOWN the page until you find verse 18. You may have to look in the next column or even on the next page before you find the 18.

Matthew 1:18 begins: "Now the ________________ of Jesus the Messiah . . . ."

verse

In the Bible reference

JOHN 3:16,

draw a circle around the CHAPTER number.

Luke

2 1

Look up the beginning of the Christmas story in your Bible.

The Bible reference is LUKE 2:1. Luke is in the New Testament.

After you find Luke, look for the big number 2. Verse 1 will not have a number, but you know it is at the beginning of Chapter 2.

The Christmas story in Luke begins:

"In those ________________ a decree went out . . . ."

John(3):16

In the Bible reference

JOHN 3:16,

draw a square around the VERSE number.

verses

The Christmas story begins with the FIRST VERSE of the SECOND CHAPTER of LUKE.

To make it shorter, you say that the Christmas story begins with LUKE 2:1

(We SAY, "Luke two, one.")

If you want to read the Christmas story in the Bible, you will look for the book named ________________, then find chapter ___________, and begin reading at verse ___________.

John 3 :16

References are written with a colon (:).

Some Bibles use periods with references (.)

Either way it means the same thing.

If you see a Bible reference like this: John 1.4, what is another way of writing it? ________________

89

chapters

90

In the Bible, the CHAPTERS have been divided into small parts called ______________________.

John 1:4

Here is a picture of Chapter 3 in the Book of John.

Find JOHN 3:16 in your Bible.

Start with the big number 3 and look until you find the verse number 16. In some Bibles, you might find this verse in the next column.

Read ALL THE WORDS of VERSE John 3:16 in your Bible.

John 2 1228

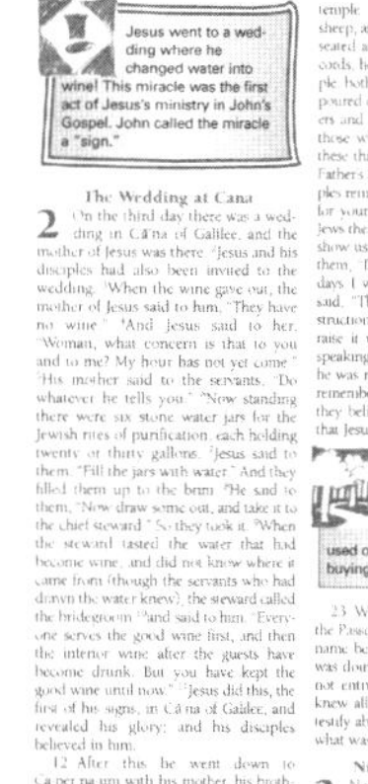

Jesus went to a wedding where he changed water into wine! This miracle was the first act of Jesus's ministry in John's Gospel. John called the miracle a "sign."

The Wedding at Cana

The Temple was built as a place for people to come and worship God through prayer and sacrifice. Jesus wanted the Temple to be used only for worship and not for buying and selling things.

Jesus Cleanses the Temple

Nicodemus Visits Jesus

1229 John 3

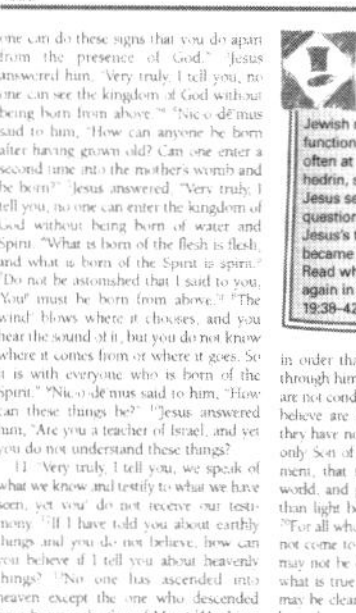

Nicodemus was a member of the Sanhedrin, a group of Jewish religious leaders who functioned as a court. Jesus was often at odds with the Sanhedrin, so Nicodemus came to Jesus secretly at night to ask questions and to hear more of Jesus's teachings. Nicodemus became a follower of Jesus. Read where he is mentioned again in John 7:45-52 and John 19:38-42.

16 "For God so loved the world that he gave his only Son, so that everyone who believes in him may not perish but may have eternal life.

17 "Indeed, God did not send the Son into the world to condemn the world, but

Jesus and John the Baptist

"For God so loved the world that he gave his only Son, so that everyone who believes in him may not perish but may have eternal life."
John 3:16

Many words can go in the blank—whatever makes sense.

find things
look up things
find verses
look up references

(Or something that means the same thing.)

In the Bible, most of the BOOKS have been divided into large parts called ______________________________.

1229 **John 3**

one can do these signs that you do apart
from the presence of God." [3]Jesus
answered him, "Very truly, I tell you, no
one can see the kingdom of God without
being born from above."[a] [4]Nic-o-dē'mus
said to him, "How can anyone be born
after having grown old? Can one enter a
second time into the mother's womb and
be born?" [5]Jesus answered, "Very truly, I
tell you, no one can enter the kingdom of
God without being born of water and
Spirit. [6]What is born of the flesh is flesh,
and what is born of the Spirit is spirit.[b]
[7]Do not be astonished that I said to you,
'You[c] must be born from above.'[d] [8]The
wind[b] blows where it chooses, and you
hear the sound of it, but you do not know
where it comes from or where it goes. So
it is with everyone who is born of the
Spirit." [9]Nic-o-dē'mus said to him, "How
can these things be?" [10]Jesus answered
him, "Are you a teacher of Israel, and yet
you do not understand these things?

11 "Very truly, I tell you, we speak of
what we know and testify to what we have
seen; yet you[e] do not receive our testimony. [12]If I have told you about earthly
things and you do not believe, how can
you believe if I tell you about heavenly
things? [13]No one has ascended into
heaven except the one who descended
from heaven, the Son of Man.[f] [14]And just
as Moses lifted up the serpent in the
wilderness, so must the Son of Man be
lifted up, [15]that whoever believes in him
may have eternal life.[g]

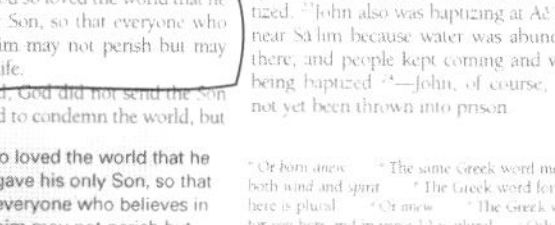

16 "For God so loved the world that he
gave his only Son, so that everyone who
believes in him may not perish but may
have eternal life.

17 "Indeed, God did not send the Son
into the world to condemn the world, but

Nicodemus was a
member of the San-
hedrin, a group of
Jewish religious leaders who
functioned as a court. Jesus was
often at odds with the Sanhedrin, so Nicodemus came to
Jesus secretly at night to ask
questions and to hear more of
Jesus's teachings. Nicodemus
became a follower of Jesus.
Read where he is mentioned
again in John 7:45–52 and John
19:38–42.

in order that the world might be saved
through him. [18]Those who believe in him
are not condemned; but those who do not
believe are condemned already, because
they have not believed in the name of the
only Son of God. [19]And this is the judg-
ment, that the light has come into the
world, and people loved darkness rather
than light because their deeds were evil.
[20]For all who do evil hate the light and do
not come to the light, so that their deeds
may not be exposed. [21]But those who do
what is true come to the light, so that it
may be clearly seen that their deeds have
been done in God."[g]

Jesus and John the Baptist

22 After this Jesus and his disciples
went into the Judean countryside, and he
spent some time there with them and baptized. [23]John also was baptizing at Ae'non
near Sa'lim because water was abundant
there; and people kept coming and were
being baptized [24]—John, of course, had
not yet been thrown into prison.

"For God so loved the world that he gave his only Son, so that everyone who believes in him may not perish but may have eternal life."
John 3:16

[a] Or *born anew* [b] The same Greek word means both *wind* and *spirit* [c] The Greek word for *you* here is plural [d] Or *anew* [e] The Greek word for *you* here and in verse 12 is plural [f] Other ancient authorities add *who is in heaven* [g] Some interpreters hold that the quotation concludes with verse 15

If your teacher says, "Matthew two, one"; or writes Matthew 2:1, he or she means:

the Book of ____________________

chapter ____________________

verse ____________________

PUT A WORD OR A NUMBER IN EACH BLANK.

REMEMBER,
NOW YOU READ ONLY
THE PAGES NUMBERED
AFTER PAGE 88.

Most of the books of the Bible have been divided into chapters, and the chapters have been divided into verses to make it easier to ______________________________ in the Bible.

Matthew

2

1

TIME TO REST!

WHEN YOU ARE READY TO GO AGAIN, TURN THE PAGE.

THEN TURN THE BOOK UPSIDE DOWN AND READ THOSE PAGES.

(BEGIN WITH PAGE 87.)

God is with us and always hears our prayers. Sometimes when we pray, we use our bodies to express the feelings behind our words. Here are some different positions, or postures, that you can use when you pray!